Mental Toughness:

6 Steps to Build the Strongest Mindset for Life and Become Totally Unstoppable!
+7 Day Mental Toughness Challenge and Assertiveness Training. Master Self Discipline!

Table of Contents

Introduction.......8
Chapter 1: What is Mental Toughness? 11
Chapter 2: How To Become Mentally Tough.......20
   Make a Decision
   Be Consistent
   Be Mindful of Your Self-Talk
   Determining What You Can and Can't Do
   Willingness to Tackle Difficult Things First
   Be Very Responsive
   Expect Pain
   Break Down Difficult Tasks into Easy-To-Digest Pieces
   Know How to Handle Stress
Chapter 3: Mental Toughness Exercises.......33
   Create Your Mental Toughness Statement
   Me+ 50 Activity
   Self-Talk Remix
   What's Under There?
   Managing Expectations
   Meditate, Meditate, Meditate
   Visualization and Simulation

Rethinking Failure
Get a Therapist
Time Accountant
Read More
Create Your Quotes List
Find Your Accountability Help
Self-Care and Stress-Management Scoop
Develop Your Emotional Intelligence and Self-Awareness
Bolster Your Weaknesses

Chapter 4: 15 Tips From Mentally Tough People.......54

Chapter 5: 7-Day Mental Toughness Challenge.......62

Chapter 6: Being Mentally Tough In Your Day-to-Day Life.......75

Marriage Scenarios
  Scenario 1
  Scenario 2
  Scenario 3
Parenting Scenarios
  Scenario 1
  Scenario 2
  Scenario 3
Work Scenarios
  Scenario 1
  Scenario 2
  Scenario 3
Family Scenarios

    Scenario 1
    Scenario 2
    Scenario 3
  Money Scenarios
    Scenario 1
    Scenario 2
    Scenario 3
  Day-To-Day Scenarios
    Scenario 1
    Scenario 2
    Scenario 3
  Visualizing Day-To-Day Scenarios
Conclusion.......124

© Copyright 2019 by Luke Caldwell - All rights reserved.

This Book is provided with the sole purpose of providing relevant information on a specific topic for which every reasonable effort has been made to ensure that it is both accurate and reasonable. Nevertheless, by purchasing this Book you consent to the fact that the author, as well as the publisher, are in no way experts on the topics contained herein, regardless of any claims as such that may be made within. As such, any suggestions or recommendations that are made within are done so purely for entertainment value. It is recommended that you always consult a professional prior to undertaking any of the advice or techniques discussed within.

This is a legally binding declaration that is considered both valid and fair by both the Committee of Publishers Association and the American Bar Association and should be considered as legally binding within the United States.

The reproduction, transmission, and duplication of any of the content found herein, including any specific or extended information will be done as an illegal act regardless of the end form the information ultimately takes. This includes copied versions of the work both physical, digital and audio unless express consent of the Publisher is provided beforehand. Any additional rights reserved.

Furthermore, the information that can be found within the pages described forthwith shall be considered both accurate and truthful when it comes to the recounting of facts. As such, any use, correct or incorrect, of the provided information will render the Publisher free of responsibility as to the actions taken outside of their direct purview. Regardless, there are zero scenarios where the original author or the Publisher can be deemed liable in any fashion for any damages or hardships that may result from any of the information discussed herein.

Additionally, the information in the following pages is intended only for informational purposes and should thus be thought of as universal. As befitting its nature, it is presented without assurance regarding its prolonged validity or interim quality. Trademarks that are mentioned are done without written consent and can in no way be considered an endorsement from the trademark holder.

Introduction

Congratulations on downloading *Mental Toughness* and thank you for doing so.

The following chapters will discuss everything you need to know about becoming mentally tough. Whether you want to be stronger and more graceful in how you handle life's disappointments, or you want to develop your already strong mind, the following chapters will help you do it! This book is written in an easy-to-understand format, so you can grasp the concepts and effectively apply them to your life. The chapter topics include the following:

In Chapter 1, all things mental toughness will be discussed. You will learn what it is and what it's not. In Chapter 2, attention will be given to what you can do to become mentally tough. The fun begins in Chapter 3, at which point, you will learn how to exercise that mental toughness muscle. Easy, simple, practical exercises will be given to help you improve your mental toughness and focus throughout the chapter. This chapter is also great at creating a strong foundation in helping you in becoming mentally tough no matter what life brings you. Chapter 4 gives great tips from mentally tough people, so you can emulate their success and hear what they have to say.

In Chapter 5, you will have the opportunity to check out the 7-day mental toughness challenge. This challenge is all about helping you jumpstart your mental toughness journey! Some of the tasks during this journey may make you feel uncomfortable, but that's okay! They are all an important step in helping you become mentally tough. Chapter 6, the very last chapter, highlights ways you can be mentally tough in your day-to-day life. It covers common scenarios that may happen on the job, in your friend and familial relationship, during a crisis, and other day-to-day situations. The fun part of this chapter helps you use some of the skills learned in earlier chapters to set you up for mental toughness success.

Ultimately, this book is chock-full of tips, advice, help, and information to support you in meeting your mental toughness goals! I can't wait to hear about all the successes that you have gained from reading this book. I guess I'll get out of the way and let you get to reading!

There are plenty of books on this subject on the market. Thanks again for choosing this one! Every effort was made to ensure it is full of as much useful information as possible. Please enjoy!

Chapter 1: What is Mental Toughness?

Mental toughness. We hear about it all the time, from spiritual leaders to politicians to sports commentators, about how people need to be mentally tough. If you want to have a successful life, then being mentally tough is a common theme that pops up over and over again. But, before anything else, what is mental toughness?

Mental toughness is simply being able to overcome obstacles in life by being preserving and able to move forward no matter how difficult the circumstances are around you or what setbacks you may encounter. Being mentally tough requires dedication to keep going for your goal by setting your mind to do whatever you set out to do and never wavering. Other terms you may have heard when referencing mental toughness can include an athlete 'being in the zone' or 'being a clutch player' when it comes to sports. Other words to describe being it would be someone who's gritty or resilient. Athletes, people in business (especially sales and management), people in the army, or anyone with a high-stress job are often considered being mentally tough. A lot of successful leaders are also considered to be mentally tough to do phenomenal things.

During the 1980s, in the Performance Psychology field, a concept known as mental toughness began to be studied. This field of psychology became known as sport psychology, and it's all about helping athletes reach their full potential by fine-tuning their mental skill so they can do exceptional things. Vince Lombardi, a former professional football player, is considered the godfather of being mentally tough because of his winning record and standard of excellence; but, being mentally tough isn't all about winning. This field of study helped extremely talented people continue to be successful once they reached their physical capabilities. What would be the best way to keep going? This is where mental toughness comes in. It helps you defy your physical limitations and trains your brain to keep going to meet your personal goals despite what appears to be insurmountable obstacles surrounding you. Being mentally tough is something that comes out during extreme circumstances; however, there are some foundational steps that you can take to become more mentally tough.

The easiest way to determine your level of mental toughness is to recall what happens when you are in tough situations. (*The great thing about this book is you do not have to say it out loud you can just think about it.*) Do you normally stop when the going gets tough? Do you find a way to blame other people if things do not go your way? Or do you keep on going no matter what the situation is? Depending on what your answer is, you can determine if you are at least a little bit mentally tough or not. The good thing is, no matter what your answer is, you can always improve your mental toughness. But before we get to that, what are the foundational steps you can take to increase your mental toughness? Keep reading to find out more.

The first step in helping you become mentally tougher is to know your personality type. There are many personality type tests that you can take to help you determine what type of personality you have. You can often take these tests for free, and you can do it at home rather quickly. It is important to know your personality type because you can then determine what steps you should take to develop your mental toughness. A popular personality test is the Jung Typology Test. A Google search will also give you more results as well.

The next foundational step you want to take is to get your self-starter mindset in gear. Normally, self-starters are considered people who tend to have a large dose of mental toughness already. The next personality trait you want to start developing to become more mentally tough is to become more self-aware. When you are self-aware, you can take out your bias in a situation and look at it with an open mind. You can look at a scenario and figure out why you did something by separating your emotions from the situation. In other words, you can begin to look at situations objectively. You can then think about ways that you would do differently to help you develop your mental toughness. No worries, we will discuss this more in chapters.

Next, you will want to know if you are a glass-half-full or glass-half-empty type of person. Do you move through life because you are optimistic about greater opportunities? Or do you move through life because you want to avoid negative outcomes? Both factors are important motivators and knowing which one you are is going to be very important and how you train your brain to be mentally tough.

Another important foundational aspect of being mentally tough is to know yourself. This is similar to being self-aware, except you do not have to worry about external factors. When you know yourself, you can determine why you do something or what is your motivation for your personal goals. What is your motivation or what do you see as your personal purpose in your life? Knowing who you are and why you do something is an integral part of being mentally tough.

Along the same line, it is also important to be able to think about your childhood. When you do so, you may realize that the things that occurred in your childhood are affecting you now and you may be able to correct some of those beliefs that are limiting you.

Now that we know what mental toughness is and the foundational considerations you should reflect upon before beginning your mental toughness journey, we will now switch gears to what mental toughness is not.

Mental toughness is not short-term; it is a lifelong pursuit. Do not get me wrong. You can use mental toughness to reach short-term goals, but it is a skill that you can come back to time and time again. It is not a one-off. The ability to continually be mentally tough is a true determination of whether you have the mental toughness muscle or not. But with any muscle or any skill, the more you use it, the better you become at it.

Mental toughness is not for the weak-minded, but the weak-minded can use it. If you are mentally tough, you are inherently not weak. You can be strong physically and still have mental toughness. It is not just for people who are strong physically. The even better news is that mental toughness is a skill that even those who have not needed to be mentally strong can develop.

Lastly, mental toughness is not bought. There are some skills you can buy like extra help to assist you at your home, like a maid or maintenance person. You can even buy the services of a hairdresser, barber, or nail technician. There are also some assets you can buy like body parts, cars, houses, and more physical assets. However, mental toughness is not one of the services or assets that can be bought. You have to work for it to gain it. To make the most of your life, you need to be mentally tough. There are no ifs, ands, or buts about it.

The rest of the book will focus on what mental toughness looks like in a lived lifestyle and how to develop this so important trait.

Chapter 2: How to Become Mentally Tough

If you think being mentally tough is extremely difficult to become, you are not entirely right, but you are not entirely wrong either. This chapter will highlight how you can become mentally tough. Think of each step to become mentally tough as a rung on a ladder. In order to reach the top of the ladder, you need to climb each step to get to the top, so the more rung you climb, the more you can make it to the top. However, you have to completely climb each step to successfully reach the top.

Why do you want to be mentally tough? The road to being mentally tough is not going to be easy. You are going to run into a lot of setbacks and challenges along the way to develop this skill that will test your limits. So, before you begin, you must know why you want to be mentally tough. Is it because you are trying to win an Olympic competition? Is it because you want to impress your parents and show that you are responsible? Or is it because you want to meet other personal, financial, mental, or spiritual goals? Whatever your reason is to become mentally tough is your personal reason, but make sure that this reason is predicated on your personal goals, beliefs, and desires and not anyone else's. If your decision is based on other people's influence or opinion, this path is not going to help you when you really need it. You have to focus on what type of person you are now, who you want to be, and the importance of being mentally tough for you to reach that goal.

Make a Decision

This is the very first step in becoming mentally tough. You have to decide to become mentally tough. This decision is cut-and-dried, and when you decide that you want to be mentally tough, you will make it. In order to climb the very first run, you need to make the easy decision of "Hey, I want to be mentally tough." Once you make that decision, everything else should fall into place. Once you make that decision, know and accept that it's not going to be easy. When you begin, you should already expect some hardship so when it comes, you will not be affected to the point that you want to give up. If it was easy being mentally tough, then everyone would do it. Cliché, I know, but it's true. So, the first rung again is to decide to be mentally tough and then don't expect the journey to mental toughness to be easy.

Be Consistent

The next step in becoming mentally tough is to be consistent. Since you already know that you want to become mentally tough, you will have to be consistent in that quest. This means that no matter what's going on around you, you need to do the same thing every day. If you are trying to develop your mental toughness to reach a personal goal, this means that you will work on your mental toughness exercises with intensity. In other words, it means you are going to do the work with intensity every day. If you are trying to develop your mental toughness in the sports arena, that means you need to practice like you are going to play in the game which means you must go hard and intense at all times in practice, so you will not be shocked when you get in the actual game. If you are in the field of sales, that means you make your sale call with the same professionalism and intensity every day as if every phone call is going to be a sale. This commitment to being consistent is the next step in being mentally tough. Being consistent means that if you are in a difficult situation that is testing your growth or preventing you from putting the work in, you will find a way to overcome that challenge and to be consistent no matter what the negativity or difficulties around you. Strive for excellence in everything that you do.

Be Mindful of Your Self-Talk

The next rung you want to take in your climb to being mentally tough is to be mindful of your self-talk. When things get tough, are you quick to shut yourself down? Are words like *I can't, I do not know, I will never be able to do that*, or other negative words in your vocabulary? Are you quick to wish that you were not doing what you are doing when an unpleasant situation arises? Do you tell yourself negative things? Or are you encouraging yourself? Are you also gentle and kind to yourself? Do you tell yourself to keep going no matter what the odds are? If you responded that you speak negatively to yourself, you have to stop. Your self-talk must change from negative to positive. To become mentally tough, you have to speak positive things to yourself. This positive thinking helps you continue to keep going when things look like they are going to fail. Those who think positive are able to succeed because they believe they can.

In the same vein, mentally tough people think positive, but they do not overthink. Sometimes, you can lose focus on the task at hand when you overthink. The overthinking becomes negative self-talk, and you are back in the negative place that you were before. Overthinking hinders you from moving forward because you are too busy thinking instead of doing. Mentally tough people make a decision confidently and stick to it. Once they make that decision, they think positively about the outcome and take the steps that are necessary to help them move forward towards their goals.

Determining What You Can and Can't Do

The next rung to climb to mental toughness is being able to determine what you can do about a situation and what you cannot do. This ability to master what you can do about something and what you are not able to do is a necessity. To become mentally tough, you must focus on what you can do and not on what you cannot do in any given situation. By giving your attention to what you can do, you are making sure that you can actually change the situation by actively changing what you can instead of wasting time on things that you cannot change.

The Memphis Grizzlies have a saying that, "We grind here.' This means that their basketball teams continue to play hard no matter who the team is. They can play against the worst team in the league and they will grind. They will play against the best team in the league and they will also grind. To be mentally tough, you must also grind. Another way to say it is to simply persevere. This means that no matter what the obstacles are, you keep going. It means that even when your body aches and you have one more rep, you get it done. It means when you are tired, and you want to go to sleep, you keep going with this commitment to grind. Grinding strengthens your mental toughness muscle.

Willingness to Tackle Difficult Things First

This is the next rung to mental toughness which means you are not afraid to handle tough situations no matter how uncomfortable they may be. Additionally, to become mentally tough, you have to know that failure is not bad; it is actually a good thing. The more you fail at your task, it helps you realize what you need to do to be successful. This ability to think about failure in a positive way is very important when you are on the path to becoming mentally tough. This helps you realize that mentally tough people keep going no matter what. Failure is only helping you get one step closer to your goal.

Be Very Responsive

The next rung you will want to master is to be very responsive. This means that no matter what happens you can adjust and be flexible. You are not stagnant, and you want to stay the same way. You know that the only constant in life is change and you are okay with that. To be mentally tough, you have to be able to go with the flow, change your game plan, and be okay with that. If you are adverse to change, you are going to have a difficult time. So, prepare your mind that you will need to change.

Expect Pain

Oh, in case I didn't say it, let me say it again. The journey to mental toughness is not going to be easy! So, the next rung to the top is to expect pain. Let me repeat it, *the journey to mental toughness is not going to be easy*. I say this because being in pain is uncomfortable and the next rung to the top is to be okay with being uncomfortable. Sometimes, being uncomfortable is a step that no one likes to take, but you have to overcome this step-in order to be mentally tough.

Break Down Difficult Tasks into Easy-To-Digest Pieces

The next and last rung that you must overcome in the climb to mental toughness is the ability to break down difficult tasks into easy-to-digest pieces. If you are training for a marathon, you are not just going to start running 13 miles. You are going to run mile by mile. And the journey to mental toughness is the same way. When you are becoming mentally tough, you go a little bit at a time until it all comes together. Next thing you know, you are handling tough situations like a pro. Another important aspect of this rung is knowing how to manage your expectations. By keeping your expectations realistic, you are able to keep going instead of being bogged down with disappointment, despair, and hurt that you are not reaching your goals as quickly as you would like.

Know How to Handle Stress

Lastly, when you are mentally tough, you know how to handle stress. This step is integral in order to be mentally tough. When things get tough, and we know they will, you will be able to cope with the stress if you know how to handle it. One of my favorite sayings is that being mentally tough is not about powering through, it is about how you recharge. How true is that! When things are stressful, it's okay to take a break, regroup, and come back to the task. That does not mean that you are failing to be strong mentally. It just means that you know your limitations and you are ready to recharge and get back to the task at hand once you have regrouped.

The journey to mental toughness is going to be hard and long, but if you go a little bit at a time and develop the necessary skills, you will be a mentally tough pro sooner than you think.

Chapter 3: Mental Toughness Exercises

This chapter is all about putting the work into becoming mentally tough. We now know what the steps are that you need to climb to reach the top of the mental toughness ladder, but what does that look like practically? This chapter gives you exercises that will help you develop the skills on being mentally tough in the previous chapter. This will help you to be able to climb the ladder to mental toughness much easier than if you do not do them. If an exercise seems difficult at first, that's okay because it is also expected. Continue to grind to get better at the activity, and you will see the results! That's how mental toughness works. You keep going at something until you get better at it.

Create Your Mental Toughness Statement

The first activity in our mental toughness exercise toolkit is to create your mission statement. In your mental toughness statement, you want to include a few questions. First, consider why do you want to be mentally tough? That should be included in your mental toughness statement. Then, you want to give yourself a time frame or a goal of when you want to see improvement with your mental toughness so that you can see some improvement within that time frame. Of course, you want to be realistic. Worst-case scenario, if you do not meet your goal, you are okay with that. This document is a living document which means it can change to meet your needs.

Lastly, you may want to sign your mental toughness statement like it's a contract so that it is legally binding to yourself. This will help you be more accountable for your actions. You will also want to store your mental toughness statement in a special place, so you can pull it out and look at it at any time or you can even put it on the wall, so you can see it all the time. You can also jazz your statement up by pulling out your calligraphy kit and writing it with your special ink or on special paper or add glitter and sparkles to the document to really make it stand out.

Me+ 50 Activity

This activity is all about helping you discover the person that you want to be. Who will you be in 50 years? What will be your hair color? What type of clothes will you wear? Where will you live? What will your family look like? What type of job will you have? Will you have any pets? Are you going to have any sickness? Will you be retired, or will you still be working? Let your imagination run wild! Write down any and everything you see yourself as a 50-year-old you, then check to see if your actions in your daily life are adding up to that. If you want to own a boat, but are not sure how to buy a boat, then research it. The more you are armed with knowledge, the more you will be able to properly take the steps to help you reach your goals.

Self-Talk Remix

The next activity is targeted towards yourself talk. Once you finish this activity, the goal is to help you consistently have more positive self-talk than negative self-talk. If you are already doing a great job with your self-talk, that's fine. You can do this activity and it will reinforce your already positive self-talk to take it to the next level. The first thing you want to do is grab a sheet of paper and a pen. Draw a line straight down the middle of the page. Then, on the left side, write down some of your most phrases you say with your self-talk. Be sure to include every single negative thing that you say even if it consists of the words *I can't*, *I won't*, or *I do not*.

Now, on the right side of the paper, write the positive version of that negative self-talk. Be sure to include positive affirming words such as *I can*, *I will*, and *I do*. Study these phrases so the next time your mind begins to say the negative self-talk, it will automatically replace the negative phrases with positive ones that you just wrote down. Every time you catch yourself with a negative self-talk phrase, add it to the list. Do this each and every time so you can start correcting itself.

Alternatively, you can also change your self-talk all together and give yourselves a new one. What you can do is create a list of affirmations. Affirmations are slight mantras that you tell yourself every day to get positive results. The same affirmations can be applied to developing your self-talk. A few mantras you can use are as follows: *You are mentally tough. You can get through a tough situation. Situations do not affect you. You are in charge of your destiny.* You can use these to get started or you can create your own.

What's Under There?

Uncovering your limited beliefs is the purpose of this next activity. In this activity, you have to take a trip down memory lane. What are two limiting beliefs that you have? A limiting belief is similar to negative self-talk. It is a belief that limits you from reaching your full capability. For example, a limiting belief can be that '*Fat people are lazy*' but that may not be the case at all. Another limiting belief could be that you are not able to make more than a certain amount of money because rich people are the devil. We all have limiting beliefs. What are yours? Write them down.

Then, go back to your earliest memory of this limiting belief. When did you first hear it? Do you have this belief because someone told you that the limiting belief was true? Or do you have the limiting belief because of something you observed in your life? Once you get to the root of why you have the limiting belief, you then will want to explore the opposite and alternate possibilities of this belief. Is it possible that your limiting belief may not be true? What would the limiting belief sound like if it was different? Do you still believe that limiting belief or has it changed for you? If so, why do you still believe it? If you do not believe that limited belief anymore, replace it with the positive version of the limited belief. So, instead of '*People who are millionaires are morally bankrupt.*" try "*People who are millionaire are not morally bankrupt.*'

Anytime you have a limited belief, go back in time to try to figure out why you got that limiting belief. Explore if you still believe it or not, and if you don't, think of what you can do to change the limiting belief to a positive one so it's not holding up your life.

Managing Expectations

We all have goals that we want to accomplish. The purpose of this activity is to break down your goals into small actionable steps. After you write down your limiting beliefs, the next thing you want to write down is your expectations. Mentally tough people manage your expectations and they can change them if they do not meet their expectations. When you write down your expectations, are they realistic? For example, if you want to be a brain surgeon but you have not been to medical school, that is not a realistic expectation.

If you want to run 13 miles but you have not even run one mile, that is not a realistic expectation. Make sure that your expectations are realistic. If the things you want to do seems too big, find a way to take steps so you can accomplish what you want to achieve. If you are not self-aware and are working on that skill, you can then reach out to someone else, like a friend or a family member or someone else that you trust, to see what they think about your expectations. But take what they say with a grain of salt to make sure that you are being true to yourself. They will most likely let you know if you are being realistic or not with your goals. Now, I'm not saying you should limit your goals. By all means, reach for the stars. Just know that if you have lofty goals, you can expect to put in a lot more work than if your goals are not as ambitious. Whatever your goals are, just be open to how they will change your life and adjust your life accordingly.

Meditate, Meditate, Meditate

Meditation is the next important activity that you should get into the habit of doing. If you haven't started yet, do it now so you can start to be in tune with yourself and be more open if you are making progress with your goals or not. Set aside 10 to 15 minutes to try and meditate every day.

Make sure that the place you select is nice and quiet. If you need to create a special place, please do so. Once you find a quiet spot and have allotted yourself time, try to make your busy thoughts calm down.

During this quiet time, you can reflect upon situations that bother you and how to handle them or meditate on outcomes that you want to achieve. To get into the habit of stilling your thoughts, you can think of your favorite calm place. You can also put on calming music to help you relax. You can slowly breathe in and breathe out to calm yourself. Then, think about the things that you have gone through or are currently going through. Sometimes, after a meditation session, you may realize some uncomfortable truths. If that happens, you need to be able to handle those truths accordingly no matter how uncomfortable or painful it may be.

If you do not want to think about your problems while doing this meditation session, you can do affirmations instead. All you have to do is to repeat them over and over again until you start seeing that your self-talk reflects that. Trust me, once you begin meditating, you will see a difference in your mental toughness!

Visualization and Simulation

Visualization is similar to meditation, except when you visualize something instead of just thinking about whatever you are going through, you actually picture it in detail. For example, if you are visualizing that you will one day own a house, in this technique, you actually imagine what the house looks like. When was it built? How is the inside decorated? What do the garden and the backyard look like? Who are your neighbors? Try to visualize what you want to accomplish as detailed and as specific as possible. Try to keep it as detailed as you can so you can watch it come to life. Also, try to keep your visualizations as positive and realistic as possible.

Rethinking Failure

Rethinking failure is the next activity. Think of some of your recent failures. Instead of focusing on why it didn't work, think about all the things that you have learned from the failure. By focusing on the knowledge that you gained from the task, you can try the new and improved steps the next time you attempt the same task. This commitment to examining what was successful in your actions and what was not successful and what you can do to improve will help you with becoming mentally tough.

Get a Therapist

This next activity may cost you some money but may be well worth it. If you feel that these activities are overwhelming or triggering your thoughts that you feel like you need some assistance exploring, you can reach out to a therapist. Some therapists do not mind helping you sit through your thoughts and figure out ways for you to become mentally tough. If you have insurance, it is part of the coverage in the insurance policy sometimes. You can check with your insurance provider to see if they will provide for the therapist free of charge or not. If you do not have insurance, there are often lots of free opportunities to get free therapy. Research for local non-profit organizations in the area that can help. If you are feeling extremely overwhelmed or suicidal, take advantage of hotlines that can help you with your mental toughness in that exact moment.

Reaching out for help is not weak; it actually means that you are very strong and mentally tough. It helps you get professional help to develop your mental toughness. Now, if you do not have the money or you don't think this stuff is necessary, that's fine. Choosing not to go to a mental therapist will not prevent you from developing your mental toughness. You can continue to develop your mental toughness by doing the suggested exercises.

Time Accountant

The next thing you want to do is you examine your time. Make a schedule of your day-to-day activities. You can manually write out the times from noon to midnight or you can print off a week-long calendar from the Internet and fill it in. For this activity, you want to be as detailed as possible, so try to account every single minute. If you cannot remember everything, that's fine. Just write what you can remember. Once you write those things down, assess your day-to-day activities and the time you spend on them. How much time do you spend doing the necessities like eating, sleeping, working, and spending time with your family? What are things you spend time on that is now helping you reach your goals?

Are you spending lots of time browsing the web, gossiping, or on social media without helping you improve your goals or without actively helping you become mentally tough? Whatever the things that are wasting your time, find a way to reduce it. Instead, spend your time on activities that will help you boost your mental toughness.

Read More

To become mentally tough, you can begin reading more. Read diversely and read things that you normally wouldn't read. This will expose you to a wide range of thinking and thoughts that will challenge your brain and bolster your knowledge. The more you know, the more you are able to handle various situations because you have a broad base of experience to draw from. You don't have to read long novels. You can read magazines or even visit websites and read articles about things you do not normally read about. You can visit any newspaper online or in the store and check out their information to read a wide range of topics.

Create Your Quotes List

Next is to create a list of quotes from your favorite mentally tough people. These quotes will help you remain mentally tough in the face of adversity. You can list them next to your mission statement, so you can have some inspiration when things get tough. You can also use social media to follow mentally tough people or those who inspire you to become one. You can start off with a list of 10 quotes and you can continue to add to the list as you find more great quotes to help you along the way.

Find Your Accountability Help

You will want to find your accountability partner. You can find that accountability partner online or in person; it can be a friend or a family member that you trust. You can also find a support group where you can encouraging each and every one, be motivated, and keep track of group progress. Having help and being accountable with your mental toughness walk will have others call you on your BS if you are not doing the necessary work to become mentally tough. You can also reach out to those you deem mentally tough to get insight and advice on how they became mentally tough so that you can apply it as well in your life.

Self-Care and Stress-Management Scoop

The next activity you want to do is to figure out a way to manage your self-care. Self-care is how you take care of yourself when things get stressful. This is important because it is part of the way you handle stress. Come up with a plan. What are you going to do when you are stressed out? Are you going to listen to a certain song or read a certain magazine or call someone? Knowing how to take care of yourself and how to manage your stress will help you be successful as you try to become mentally tough. When you are disappointed, you do not want to wallow in your self-pity because it prevents you from moving forward. Mentally tough people handle situations head-on and find a way to resolve the issue.

Develop Your Emotional Intelligence and Self-Awareness

Being emotionally intelligent and self-aware are both important aspects of being mentally tough. Being emotionally intelligent boils down to this: you want to make sure that you are being empathetic to everyone you meet no matter what the situation is and learning how to treat others how you want to be treated at all times. Being self-aware is being extremely cognizant of how others perceive you, whether that perception is true or not, and then react accordingly. Being self-aware on a personal level is being in tune with your limitations and being honest about the situation at hand. This is a skill best practiced every day. Both of these skills work in conjunction with each other to help you gain a clear picture of whatever you are facing so you are not acting blindly.

Bolster Your Weaknesses

This is an offshoot of being self-aware, but this requires you to grab a pen and paper again. Draw a line in the middle of the paper. You can also use a phone as well. Set aside 20 minutes, and then list the weaknesses that you have on the left side. On the right side, write how you are supplementing your weaknesses or finding a way to improve them or pairing them with a solution, so this is not a drain on your mental toughness journey. For example, having a bad temper may be your weakness. One way to bolster that weakness is to enroll in anger management classes. You can also try to form a strategy when you get upset, like taking 10 deep breaths so you won't lose control. No matter how big or how small the weakness is, if you can find a way to bolster it, you will be that much stronger.

Now that your rungs to mental toughness are being reinforced with these activities, we are going to hear next from mentally tough people. The tips they will give you are straight from the source and offers valuable insights on how to be mentally tough. The following advice is not speculation. It is tried and true advice that real-life people have used to become more mentally tough in their life.

Chapter 4: 15 Tips from Mentally Tough People

I love hearing from people about how they have developed their mental toughness muscle because it shows that this skill is indeed learned, and it can become stronger with the habits that you follow. While these people are anonymous, you can always get extra support and advice from people that you deem mentally tough by asking them what they did to reach this point. Most people are more than willing to share their advice and insights to people who are eager to learn, so do not be afraid to reach out.

1. Stop drinking too much caffeine. If you are a coffee lover like me, this is hard. Mentally tough people do not rely on caffeine because it causes adrenaline to pump heart in your body. This means that

the when it is time to make tough decisions for a caffeine-addicted person, you may not be able to make the clearest decision as possible. By getting rid of caffeine, you can tap into your full thoughts at any time and not be reliant upon a stimulant.

2. Be okay with spending time all by yourself. When you are spending time by yourself reflecting upon various scenarios and being self-aware about how you reacted to a situation, it fine tunes your mental toughness muscle. Likewise, when you can be by yourself, without feeling bored or lonely, it only makes you mentally tougher because you are able to reflect more in your zone and can take advantage of the power of solitude.

3. Do not take things personally. This is almost the same as do not linger in the past. If something happens, learn from it

and move on. There is no reason to stay in a constant state of sadness. In your life, you will meet crazy people and they can be hard to handle. But if you spend most of your time taking things personally, you will never be happy. Try to understand them and learn some coping skills. Focus on the future but learn from the past in order to have the best future possible.

4. Say no to things that are not helping you to move forward with your goal. If something is not important to your time, say no and move on. Do not be afraid to hurt someone's feelings by saying it. The quicker you learn how to say no, the more time you free up for yourself and your mental toughness. Know what you are about and do not let other people dictate your actions.

5. Be optimistic but be realistic. This doesn't mean that you are being a pessimist, it just means that you do not waste time on unattainable goals. Hedge your optimism with a dose of reality at all times.

6. Learn more. Whatever you are trying to be mentally tough at, learn more about it. The more you learn, the more you are better able to handle the challenges that come with your task.

7. Be nice to yourself. If you do not meet your goals, do not beat yourself up about it. No one is perfect. If you beat yourself up about whatever you miss, you may just fall even more. Remember, you have to live with yourself, so at least be able to handle yourself if necessary. Be gentle with yourself and give yourself time to develop. Nothing great happens overnight.

8. Change the scenery of your life. Sometimes, when you feel like you are in a rut, it is okay to change the scenery that will help you become more adaptable. You can go on a trip, to the park, or anywhere that is new, so you do not have to deal with the mundaneness of what you are going through. Sometimes, the change in scenery can help trigger a new thought or a new burst of energy so you can finish the task at hand.

9. Learn how to juggle. Learning how to juggle helps you develop something different. It also makes your brain become good at multitasking. Becoming a multitasker is a great skill to have to become mentally tough because you are able to juggle different things without breaking a sweat. Get it? Juggle.

10. Go as hard as you can even when you think you have reached your limit. This means that when others are struggling because you are already used to a high-intensity level, you will be miles ahead of them.

11. Do not compare yourself to others. If you do so, you are only setting yourself up for not being mentally tough. As a matter of fact, comparing yourself to others is the number one way to be depressed. Other people are not you, so do not waste your time and happiness comparing. If you have a weakness, be aware of it and find a way to improve your weakness quickly. Always remember this: you are one-of-a-kind!

12. Be happy for other people. I think the young kids say, do not be a hater. This is so true. When you have thriving people

around you, it is only an indicator of your future success.

13. Do not expect the world to owe you anything or expect anything from anyone else. Fair is whatever happens to you. Do not play the victim because no one likes a whiner. Also, being a victim takes away your power. Stay strong and remember that someone always has it rougher than what you think you have.

14. Be okay with change. Let me quote what Benjamin Disraeli said: "*Change is inevitable. Change is constant.*" The only constant in life is change. The sooner you realize it, the sooner you will be able to thrive at this thing called life. Change isn't a bad thing; it is the only thing.

15. Do not complain. No one really cares anyway. When you think of the

complainer, what do you think about? Do not be that person. You do not want people to have negative thoughts about you, so do not complain.

Chapter 5: 7-Day Mental Toughness Challenge

Now that you understand what mental toughness is, the traits of mental toughness, and the skills to exercise that tool, you need to leap into being mentally tough.

However, how to start is a question that many people ask. No need to worry, though. We can help you get started. You can jumpstart your journey to mental toughness here.

Each day has a few activities you can try to exercise one of your skills in order to become mentally tough. You can try what you want or try each and every one of the tasks. A hodge-podge of the activities focuses on making you uncomfortable as well as pushing you to the physical limit. If you can do new things and manage your reactions to them, then you are well on your way to becoming mentally tough.

You can also use and reuse these tasks as needed.

Day 1	• Take a different route home than what you usually take. Try to go the long way if you normally go the short way or vice versa. If you drive, take public transportation. No matter how you get home, switch it up.

- Eat a different meal than you usually eat. Try a different cuisine or you can change the order of the meals. Have a dinner at breakfast time or lunch for dinner as an example.
- Take a cold shower. This will definitely help prepare your mind to overcome physical conditions. The more you do something that makes you uncomfortable, the easier it will be.
- Have a no-complaining day. On this day, make no complaints. Instead of focusing on why you are upset, focus on what you can do to make the most of the situation of what you can change.

- Be grateful. Make a list of all the things that you are grateful about. This will help you always see the good side no in no matter what you do.
- Figure out your why. Think about what motivates you. Is your primary motivation fear or failure or the hope of a better future? Whatever your reason that makes you tick, be mindful of them and be sure to address any limiting beliefs you may have.
- Visit a church that you normally do not visit. You can also live-stream a different religious service that you do not usually partake. You can also read about a different religion if that's easier.

Day 2	<ul><li>Create a list of 5 affirmations that can help you in your day-to-day life. You can repeat these to yourself throughout the day or during your meditation time.</li><li>Hook up your meditation space. Re-create the special place that you will meditate at and fix it up. You can add a candle, a picture, a rug, or your favorite pillow to mark the spot.</li><li>Ask for feedback at work or from a family member or a friend on how you can improve. However, when they give you their feedback do not try to explain yourself. Only nod and say thank you and think about what they said and how you can improve.</li></ul>

	- Buy a nice journal that can help you with your reflection habits. If you are off to a slow start with meditating, you can just free-write your thoughts during your meditation time. - Think about your self-talk, what type of things do you usually tell yourself. You can use the activity in the exercises chapter in order to improve your self-talk.
Day 3	- Imagine that the worst thing that can happen to you happens to you. How do you react to it? Do a little role-play about how you can react. Give yourself different reactions. - Try to live in the moment. Whatever you are doing for the day, focus on the task at hand

without being distracted by other things. If you are always multitasking, this can be difficult, but it will help you focus in intensely on what you are doing.

- Think about your early disappointments in your life, especially during childhood. Are some of those experiences still affecting you to this day? How can you reframe them to be positive?
- Wear your hair in a different hairstyle. You can try a different part, or you can try a different hair color or just cut all your hair. For the tame people, you can try a hat or a cool hair accessory.

	- Listen to a genre of music that you have never listened to before. Try to listen to 3-5 songs. - Take a break. Whatever you are doing that is stressing you or draining your energy, just say no and take a break from it.
Day 4	- Re-evaluate your life honestly. What are your goals, values, and priorities? How does your current life align with those values? If your life is not on track with the moves you are trying to make, how can you change it? - Pick out a workout routine on YouTube and commit to working out for a month without missing a day.

- Examine your daily schedule. What are the habits or things that you do that waste your time? Try to limit those activities until you no longer do them.
- Figure out a way how you can eat healthier. Whether it is a new diet or intermittent fasting, make a commitment to be healthy and follow-through. This will only make other aspects of your life stronger.
- Commit to be as focused as you can at work for the day. Then, figure out how you can keep that pace on a regular basis. You can work in short bursts of 20 minutes, so you can maintain the pace throughout the day.

Day 5	- Think about all the things that you blame yourself for. Write them down and burn them. Let the flames represent you forgiving yourself. Let the past stay in the past. Today is a new day, so relish in it.
- Listen to a radio station that you do not normally listen to on your commute to work. It can be talk radio or a different genre. You can also try a brand-new podcast as well.
- Listen to a political station that you normally do not listen to for a day. Put yourself in the other party's shoes to see if you can have some empathy or understand why they believe what they believe. Then, try to be more compassionate.

	• If you are having a personal issue with someone, speak to them directly and calmly about the issue. Instead of letting the issue fester, address it directly and smoothly. If you are unable to control your emotions, try writing a letter or email. Mentally tough people handle issues directly. • Forgive someone who has offended you whether they know they have offended you or not. Call them and let bygones be bygones.
Day 6	• Pick out your very top fear. Face it head-on. If you are scared of spiders, go to the pet store and look at a spider. If you are scared of heights, visit a

	skyscraper. Know that you are going to be scared, but figure out a way how to be ok with the feat and cope? • What is something that you can be more consistent in doing? Start back doing that task today. • Review your stress management plan. How can you improve your strategy to handle stress better? • Give up coffee, alcohol for the day. Substitute it with water or other non-stimulating drinks. • Visit a pet shelter. By focusing on animals, you can put your life into perspective. Who knows? You may even adopt one.
Day 7	• Write your obituary. Then, begin to live like a person

worthy of the obituary you just wrote.

- What things can you improve upon to make your week better? Make it happen. Make the necessary modifications to have a better week and make each subsequent week better by doing a weekly review.
- Create a mental toughness board. Include your favorite quotes and pictures of people who are your mental toughness inspirations. Jazz it up and hang it in your special place.
- Research a therapist and consult with them for at least one session. See if your area has a local program for free therapy sessions. You can also check for

free therapy apps that can also help if you are concerned about privacy.
- Get enough sleep for the night so your brain can be clear. Sleep is an often-overlooked aspect of mentally tough people. Remember, it is not about powering through, it is about recharging. Sleep is a necessary part of the recharge process.

Chapter 6: Being Mentally Tough in Your Day-to-Day Life

Congratulations on committing to doing the work in order to become mentally tough! However, when life comes at you fast, you have to try to remember to be mentally tough instead of reverting to old habits. So, how can you be mentally tough in your every-day life without reverting? One way is to practice, but even then, there is no guarantee that you will not make mistakes. The most important thing to remember is that even if you make a mistake, you should get right back on your mental toughness horse and ride again. The purpose of this chapter is to help you figure out how you are going to handle techniques when they come at you by partaking in a little visualization and roleplay.

Different scenarios will be listed here. You will have options to choose from on how you would handle the situation. The scenarios addressed are going to be dealing with marital issues, job issues, children issues, money issues, and random issues that happen in our day-to-day life. Then, some insight will be given on how to handle a particular situation. This insight will also draw on some mode of thought and techniques used by in military, martial arts, sports, and business psychology world when giving insight about a particular scenario.

There is no right or wrong answer. You may find that you would actually do a combination of some of the actions listed, and that's fine as well. The exercises are designed to help you in various situations better by practicing mental toughness. To get more value from the exercise, focus on what answer you would choose and why you would choose it. Then, examine the answers that you would not choose, and why they would not work.

Marriage Scenarios

Let's face it. Marriage is very hard. If marriage wasn't difficult, then the divorce rate would not be over 50%. The high divorce rate shows that people are just not being mentally tough when it comes to their relationship. However, by focusing on the mental toughness aspect of your attitude, you can better handle marriage and the challenges that come with it. One of my favorite quotes is that you cannot control what happens to you, but you can control how you react to it. There has never been a truer statement in regards to marriage. Unfortunately, a lot of us are not able to control how we react to unpleasant situations in a nice way. Mental toughness helps fine-tune your response to issues that arise in your marriage. Hopefully, these scenarios will help you think and help you have a better marital relationship.

Scenario 1

Your significant other wants to do something that you do not want to do. You have mentioned that you do not want to do this, but your spouse has not listened to you at all. How should you respond?

A. You should patiently explain why you do not want to do whatever it is. After explaining, you should suck it up and go ahead and do what your spouse wants to do anyway.

B. You should sulk and do what your spouse wants to do anyway.

C. You should be honest with your spouse about your reasons for not wanting to do the said activity. Then, try to convince them about why you do not want to do it and refuse to do so.

D. You should find some sort of compromise. Make a deal of the said activity, then they will have to do something they do not want to do with you at a later time.

Insight: In martial arts psychology, an important lesson that is taught is to build up your self-esteem. When you have high self-esteem and the need comes for you to make your voice known and heard, you will be able to do so. In a situation like this, depending on your relationship dynamics, any of one of these could be the right answer. The most appropriate response is to make sure that you make your voice known in a respectful way and that it is heard, and then figure out the best thing to do afterward.

Scenario 2

You and your significant other are going through financial hardships. Your spouse has an idea that can help turn a profit, but you do not want to make any risky moves at the time. What should you do? (This scenario can be switched in that you have the idea and your spouse does not want to listen.)

A. You should give your spouse a presentation, so you can convince them that your idea is the best thing to do. Then, when you are convinced, you can do what you need to do.
B. You should do what you want to do anyway. Forgiveness is easier to get them

permission. When you make all the money, your spouse will thank you.

C. You should ask your spouse to look up the prospect together and then you guys can compromise and make the best decision that you both are comfortable with.

D. You need to focus on tried-and-true methods of reducing your debt load and focus on ways to keep going.

Insight: A major factor in business psychology is looking at controlled risk and taking the risk. Finances are one of the main reasons that relationships do not last. If you are more adventurous than your spouse or vice versa, it is important that every aspect of the financial situation is to be examined before you make a decision. Mental toughness is all about hanging in there when times get hard.

Obviously, being in a financially-difficult situation is not ideal. Since how you got there is in the past, you now have to move on your next step, which will be able to determine if you can handle the risk of an investment or not. It is up to you and your spouse to figure out how much risk you and your spouse can or cannot handle together and proceed from there. The main concern should be if the investment goes well, are you both going to be able to live with the consequences? On the flip side, if the investment goes bad, will you be able to handle the consequences as well?

In other words, examine the situation from every angle and then make the decision that's best for you both. You can try to take the opposite position and play devil's advocate, so you can get to the best solution as possible.

Scenario 3

Your child, it can be a fur baby or a human baby, is misbehaving. Your significant other wants to handle the situation one way and you want to handle it another way. Unfortunately, the behavioral issue has been going on for a long time and no matter what type of discipline you both do, the issue seems not to be improving. You both are frustrated, and you need results to get peace of mind. What should you do?

A. Since your significant other's approach to discipline has not been working, you should focus on ways you can improve the issue and not worry about what they say. Obviously, what they have said has not been working, so anything is better than what they say.

B. You should defer to your significant other. That way, if the option they choose does not work, the blame will not be on you. After their way fails, then you can finally do what you know is the right thing to do in the situation.

C. You should set a timeline with your spouse about how long it should take before you guys need to see improvements. You and your spouse should also bring the child into the situation and try every single option before you give up. If you do not see improvement within that timeline, then you should seek professional help.

D. You should rule with an iron fist. It may not be ideal and may be uncomfortable, but in the end, your baby and your spouse will thank you.

Insight: The military specializes in breaking its cadets down in training camp to see how well they will do in real-life situations. The interesting thing about military training is that it is not the people who are the smartest or the most talented that succeed in training. It is the people who have the most grit or the die-hard perseverance to get through the training. In the situation, you may have to try a softer approach, or an iron fist may be necessary depending on the child's personality. It is up to you to figure that out. Whatever you do, you will have to make sure that your spouse feels comfortable with the option.

Parenting Scenarios

This brings us to our next section. How do you deal with the challenges that come with raising kids? They are living in an ever-changing and more complex world from that before. Many tried-and-true methods of back in the day will not work on today's generation. Therefore, you are basically parenting from scratch in a highly technological world. Often, your children know more than you in regard to technology, but you have to establish some type of authority in the relationship, so your kids know that you are the parent.

How can you be mentally tough when handling them as well as preparing them to be mentally tough by your example. The following examples should help you work through some typical examples that may happen.

Scenario 1

Your child is having issues with another child at school. After encouraging your child to reach out to the teacher, the issue persists. Once you look into the issue further, you realize that this child is the child of someone that you do not like, and you would rather not have a confrontation with their parent. Deep down inside, you know if you address their child's behavior with the parent, the situation can escalate quickly. How can you handle this situation?

A. You schedule a meeting with the teacher of the two children, the other child's parents, and a school administrator to make sure everyone's needs our address.

B. You reach out to the parent with a third party to try and get to the bottom of the matter. Then, you invite the parent and the child over for dinner with the third party to see if the issue can be resolved in a more relaxed environment.

C. You send an email or note respectfully explain the situation to the child's parents, so you can reach a written agreement. Then, you continue to encourage your child to be respectful and report any instances that continue to occur. You also try to get an understanding of your child's issue to make sure that they are not the ant agonizer in this situation.

D. You fight fire for fire and stand up for your child. Sometimes, being a bully is the only language that other bullies understand.

Insight: People are sensitive about their children. And in this case, it is important to practice the utmost discipline and try not to get upset. The military is all about training people to be calm under intense pressure even life-threatening pressure. And we know that the issues surrounding one's child can trigger a life-threatening reflex. Whatever you do in this situation, make sure you come up with a plan to address your child action and the other child's actions, so they will be able to have a successful school year moving forward.

Scenario 2

You notice that your child is becoming sneakier and sneakier because your significant other is too strict (you may be the strict one). Instead of just telling you the truth, the child will not tell the truth and denies that they are doing anything wrong. And neither one of you wants to change your parenting style. How should you address your child misbehavior while getting the support of your spouse?

A. You should let your child know that you used to be a child to and that everything that they are doing, you have already done, so they do not need to try it. Then you should get your spouse to back you up no matter what.

B. You should gather proof that your child misbehavior, so they cannot deny it, and then let them know that if things do not change serious consequences will happen. Let them know that your spouse agrees with you, so you can put on a united front.

C. You should try a different approach with your child. Try to get to the bottom of why they're doing what they are doing or why do they feel that your expectations are too strict. If you understand them better, you may be able to come to a compromise.

D.   You should let your spouse handle it and then get them to let you know what happens.

Insight: As children grow older, it is natural that they want to assert their independence. However, it is still up to you as a parent to guide them in the way that they should go. With a situation like this, you would want to take a cue from martial arts psychology and that they practice situational awareness. Being situationally aware helps you know whether you need to defend yourself from attack or not. And in a situation like this, you need to be situationally aware of what's going on with your child, and then you can determine what's the best offense or defense to use in a way that will be able to address your child issue and bring your spouse on board.

Scenario 3

Your child is playing in a little basketball league team. Your child practices really hard, but they are not good at all. Despite not being any good, your child loves to play basketball. The coach is very fair and lets your child play even though your child is not as good as the other children. Thankfully, the team is very good and finds themselves advancing to the finals. In the championship game, your child's team loses, and you notice that other children begin to scapegoat your child. How do you handle the situation?

A. You let your child's cry and show them tough love they will get over it.
B. You immediately call the coach and let the coach know what's going on. Then, you get your child to quit crying and ask the teammates what's going on.

C. You do not do anything but focus on letting your child handle their reaction to the situation instead of what they do.
D. You take your child off the team and tell them that not everyone is going to like them.

Insight: Sometimes it is difficult to let your child face a tough situation. When you hover over your child too much, you have the potential of becoming a helicopter parent. In sports psychology, there is a focus on having a winner's mentality.

Being a winner can mean different things, so it is important to discuss what this means to your child. Your team may have lost the game, but are their personal goals that they won, like not tripping during a game or practicing good sportsmanship. Of course, some people feel strongly about not developing weak children by giving out participation trophies, so if you are going to make your child aware of their physical incapabilities at the moment, be sure to be tactful while doing so. The talk may actually provide a way for you to discuss other things.

For example, in sports psychology, there is also a focus on practicing every day to build championship habits. You would also consider evaluating your child's practicing habits. Lastly, there is also important to be realistic. Because children are still developing and growing, your child could have potential and they may also not be as good at the sport either. This will be a good time to discuss realistic expectations as well as how to handle tough situations without hovering over your child and giving them a chance to learn and space to develop mental toughness of their own.

Work Scenarios

We spend most of our time at our jobs. So, it is important to have some type of peace of mind at your job. It is also important to properly navigate your emotions at your job, so you can have a way to provide for your family. Unfortunately, most people have jobs that are not without challenges. As a matter of fact, it seems like most people absolutely hate their jobs. The only reason they are working is to provide for their family. The trick to maintaining some type of sanity and peace at your job is to practice mental toughness. Doing so will prevent you from losing your job and help you to have the most effective and beneficial workplace as possible. The following situations can help you with tough situations that may happen on the job. Review how you react to them.

Scenario 1

You have a new boss. But this boss is lazy and a narcissist. There is a big project coming up and your job is riding on it. However, for this job, you have to work with your boss. How do you handle this situation?

A. You just quit and tell your boss off before you do. Then, you knock everything off your boss' desk before you leave.
B. You suck it up and bear it in order to save your job. You know that this is only a short while to suffer and you really need your job, so you do so.
C. You discuss the issues that you are having with your boss in a respectful way. Then, try to make the most of the situation.
D. You bring in a third party or speak with your boss' boss in order to handle the situation and then work on doing the project as best that you can do.

Insight: In the military, being uncomfortable is a skill and aspect of mental toughness that must be developed as quickly as possible. Being comfortable with being uncomfortable is key to a situation like this. Since you are working every day to become the person you want to be, you have to handle this situation the way you best self would. Depending on if you even want this job, you have to figure a way to make your discomfort known as well as completing the project. You can also just suck it up and bear it so you do not have to deal with repercussions from your complaining. Whichever option you choose, be sure that you can handle it.

Scenario 2

There is a new position at work, but you are currently not qualified for the job. However, you will be qualified in the near future. You are taking online courses that will put you in the running for the job, but you have to wait until you finish the final test in order to get the certificate to show that you are qualified. While browsing the job description, you see a line that strictly says do not apply if you are not qualified and that your application will automatically be rejected if you should apply without being qualified. What should you do?

A. You should apply anyway and let the human resources department know the circumstances surrounding your application before you apply. You should also go ahead and put the info on your résumé, so they know that you will be qualified soon.
B. You should address the reason why you applied although you are currently not qualified in your cover letter and apply anyway.
C. You should not apply and just wait for a new position when you are qualified. You can wait for the next application to open.

D. You should contact the people before applying to make sure that it is okay to apply.

Insight: In business psychology, there is a saying that you need to fake it until you make it. In this situation, that may be a concept that could be applicable. However, you have to decide if that is something you want to do or not. Your personality will determine how you react to this situation, but no matter what happens you have to be flexible to the outcome.

Scenario 3

The entire office is swamped, and you have a particularly tough deadline to meet. However, you have an important pre-arranged appointment that you cannot miss. If you miss the appointment, you will not be able to reschedule the appointment for a while. If you go to the appointment, you will not be able to complete your work. Everyone else is swamped as well and there is absolutely no one who will take your workload. What should you do?

A. Forget about the pre-arranged appointment. You will beg and please for them to reschedule. If they are unable to reschedule, then you should just wait until next year to reschedule it.
B. Do not worry about your workload. The office knew that you had a pre-arranged appointment beforehand, so you should not be held liable for something out of your control.
C. Communicate with your boss and let them know the situation. Then, see what can be done in this situation.
D. Just grin and bear the difficulty of the situation. Try to get as much of your work done as soon as possible. Then beg and plea for help on the items that you cannot

complete. You can even offer bribes if it will help you get your workload met.

Insight: To become a better athlete, sports psychologist, or athletes tackle the hardest thing first in their workouts. And in a situation like this, no matter what option you choose, it is going to be a difficult decision. The key is to tackle the most difficult thing first. Then, communicate effectively and handle let the cards fall as they may.

Family Scenarios

Family, oh, family. You can't choose your family. Family has a special way of pushing our buttons, and sometimes you have to be mentally tough in order to handle them. Some family members are very good at being fair and diplomatic and other family members act like they would treat you like a stranger on the street. Worse as a matter of fact. The tricky part about navigating familial relationships is that you will still be family after all is said and done. Therefore, you must still have some semblance of a relationship when handling tricky scenarios. The key to lots of messy situations when dealing with family members it to communicate well. (Isn't that the key to most things in life?) Review these scenarios to see how you can react.

Scenario 1

Your family is planning a large family gathering. However, there is a dispute about how the money needs to be handled. One group wants it to be handled one way and another group wants it to be handled another way. By chance, you find yourself becoming the spokesperson for everyone and being caught up right in the middle. How would you handle this situation?

A. You will find a way to hear everyone's concerns and then bring everyone together to vote on the issue.
B. You will find a way to make the process more collaborative, so everyone's voices can be heard. You will then make the best decision to keep the peace.
C. You will say one thing and be strong, but then say your real opinion out of the spotlight so no one's feelings will get hurt.
D. You will back down because no one appointed you to be in charge of the family

event. Everyone needs to put in the work since it is a group event. You will politely tell them that you do not want to be in charge since you cannot bear all the responsibility for an event that you did not ask to be in charge of. Then, you will let the cards fall as they may.

Insight: Mentally tough people do not play the victim. It is important to remember not to play the victim in this case and to step up and communicate what you want from the situation. Sometimes, families tend to rely on one person to do all the work when there are many capable people to do whatever task is at hand. This will be a great opportunity to share the leadership roles and to let other people shine so people can feel needed and wanted. According to business psychology, one of the greatest things you can ask someone is to help them in order to meet your bottom line and to meet your goal as a team.

Scenario 2

One of your favorite cousins who is the same age as you has recently really prospered in life. This cousin has many of the things in life that you have wanted but you have not attained. When the holidays come around, your favorite cousin wants to come and hang out with you, but you are not sure how you feel about that. How would you respond?

A. You will avoid the cousin. You won't pick up his or her phone calls or respond to his or her texts or emails, so you do not have to face his or her success and look at how beautiful your life is.

B. You will accept the invitation to your cousin and let him or her know how you truly feel. You will let your cousin know that you are a little jealous of his or her success and that he or she is taking everything that you want in your life.

C. You will be happy for your cousin and see if he or she can let you in on some of the steps that he or she has taken to reach his or her goals after you have accepted the invitation. Then, you will get your cousin to pay for dinner

D. You will put a smile on your face and hang out with your cousin, but you will bring someone else, so you do not have to hang out with him or her by yourself.

Insight: Being happy for others is an important part of being mentally tough. When you are happy for others, it allows you to focus on your capabilities and not be bogged down with jealousy. Mentally tough people especially in business focus on what they can change and what they cannot change. No matter what the reason is for you not reaching your personal goals, it is not anyone else's fault. Only you are in charge of changing your destiny. In a situation like this, you should try to consider how what or what you can learn from your cousin in order to thrive as well. Finally, do not look at your cousin's success as something bad. When people around you are thriving, it is a good indicator that you will soon thrive as well.

Scenario 3

There is one family member that no one likes, but this family member does not know that. This family member overheard someone talking about him or her and becomes distraught. He or she comes to you upset because he or she did not like what he or she has heard. This family member is crying and feels betrayed. What should you tell this cousin?

A. You should be honest with your cousin and give him or her the cold, hard truth.

B. You should try to figure out why your cousin is upset and then encourage him or her to address the person that has the issue with him or her. But, no matter what you do, you should stay out of it.

C. Let that cousin know that not everyone likes him or her and it is okay. Explain that not everyone is going to like you in life, including family members. Help your cousin focus on the positive things that he or she has going on for his or her in life.

D. Let your cousin cry and act like you do not know what's going on. It is the best way to keep peace in the family.

Insight: Sometimes people talk about each other and you find yourself caught up in the middle of it if you do not set boundaries. That's exactly what mentally tough people do. They are accountable to themselves and to others, so people know not to cross the line around them.

In a situation like this, there are many different options you can take. However, you have to be the judge and encourage your cousin to be resilient. Encourage your cousin not to let other people's opinions of him or her stop him or her from being the best person that he or she can be. And, if the reason that he or she is not liked is that of a personal fault, you can always kindly draw his or her attention to the matter.

Money Scenarios

Money, money, money! Money is something that we all wish we had more of. And it is something that many people struggle with. Lots of money issues stem from the fact the people are unable to be disciplined and mentally tough with their finances. In these scenarios, you will be able to figure out or think through how to handle money issues. You will also be able to see how you can exercise some of the traits of mental toughness in order to get the most favorable outcome.

Scenario 1

You are currently on a budget. However, there is a cool up-to-date gadget that you must have. It is on sale, and the sale is a limited sale. You feel like this sale will never ever come on again. So, you break your budget and splurge on the gadget. What should you do once you get the gadget home?

A. You should take it back for buyer's remorse. Then, put the money you receive back into your bank account. This time when you put the money back into your bank account, you will not touch the money unless it is according to your budget.
B. You should try to sell the gadget for a higher price that you got it. Then, try to get some of the money back and use the profit to buy a different gadget.

C. You should enjoy it. Just because you are on the budget does not mean that you cannot enjoy yourself occasionally.
D. Enjoy the purchase and get back on track with the next issue.

Insight: Money issues can cause a level of uncomfortableness. Actually, it can cause an extreme level of discomfort. Not having money is never fun. However, in order to dig yourself out of a rough spot, you do have to be uncomfortable. In military and sports psychology, there is a principle that you should not take shortcuts for instant gratification. And a situation like this, depending on how dire the financial need is, you may want to consider returning the purchase to get your money back and just delay your gratification longer. Or you can also follow a principal and martial arts psychology that discusses getting back on track after you make a mistake. The choice is yours.

Scenario 2

Someone who owes you money asks to borrow some more from you. This time, the amount that they want to borrow is more than the original amount that they asked to borrow. What should you do?

A. You should try to ask them about the money that they owe you before giving them the money to borrow.
B. Say yes and let them know that when they pay you back to pay them the other money as well.
C. If they really need the money, you can give it to them, but if they do not need the money, then do not give it to them.
D. Just say no. Block their phone number and ignore all correspondence from them until they give you your money back.

Insight: It is important to see the best in people, but it is also important to be realistic according to military psychology. In a situation like this, you can only judge someone based on what they have shown you. However, there is also a saying in mental psychology that you should let the past be the past. If you give them money and they do not pay you back, you have to be okay with that. If they give you the money and they pay you back plus a little bit extra, you have to be ok with that, too. Whatever decision you make, you want to make sure that is in line with what you want to do in your personal goals and that giving someone else money is not putting yourself in a tight spot.

Scenario 3

Your friends are planning a trip and you have no money to go, but you really, really want to go because you have been wanting to go to this place. You think you should delay your gratification in order to save for other things, but this is a once-in-a-lifetime opportunity and you do not want to miss it. What should you do?

A. You should work overtime and miss some family time until you are at the point where you have the funds, so you can go on this amazing trip.
B. You should just forget about the trip and get them to send you pictures. You should also avoid the temptation by removing yourself from the thread about the trip.
C. You should go and just make up the tight spot when you get back in time. All work and no play are not fun.
D. You can take out a loan from a payday loan or ask to borrow the money from a friend or family member and pay them back once you get the money.

Insight: Delayed gratification is an important component of being mentally tough in all types of psychology. On the flip side, the family is one thing that many people value in a situation like this you have to determine if the trip is worth more than your long-time goals. Even if you can't make the trip, perhaps, there is something else that you can do. However, if you do take the trip, you have to make sure that you find a way to cover your expenses without compromising your long-term goals. If there is a way to do both, perhaps the trip will be possible. If not, you may have to say no.

Day-To-Day Scenarios

Life brings many situations that are troublesome. Day-to-day disappointments can be frustrating and slowly wear on you. Sometimes, the scenarios are so short, one wonders if you should even address them or not. Sometimes, you have to decide if you want to address the issue that's bothering you or let it slide. Oftentimes, your reaction to these types of situations have no semblance of mental toughness insight and depend more on how you are feeling for the day. The scenarios and this section cover random things that may happen to us all but mentally tough people react to these situations differently than the average person.

Scenario 1

In the middle of traffic, someone cuts you off. This person has been tailing you the entire time you got on the highway. Oh, yeah, you have had a very rough day. How should you handle this situation?

A. You should ignore them and continue to drive.
B. You should get really close and do the same thing to them.
C. You should focus on the music that you are listening to take your mind off the displeasure you have.

D. You should try to be nice and help them figure out what's going on. Or you can report them to the police.

Insight: Mentally tough people handle crazy drivers in a different way than non-mentally tough people do. A principle of being mentally tough is to be self-aware. While road rage is never justified, are you driving well? Are you following the rules of the law? If so, you should focus on what you can control and ignore everything else. Sometimes, knowing what battles to fight is very important and letting the past be the past is even more important. If you can get to your destination without any hurt harm or danger, then perhaps is no reason to be concerned with the momentary moment of displeasure.

Scenario 2

There is a rude person at your favorite convenience store. Every time you see them, they are rude today. You had an especially rough day today, and they are continuing with their rude ways. What should you do?

A. You should let them be rude and hurry up with your transaction, so you do not have to deal with them.
B. You should let the manager know. Let them know that every time you visit the store, they act this way.
C. You should leave feedback on a survey on the back of your receipt. You should also leave a scathing online report.
D. You should continue to kill them with kindness. It is only a few seconds of your life that you have to deal with them.

Insight: Dealing with rude people is something we all have experienced, and we all have issues with it. Okay, maybe I'm speaking for myself. But in a situation like this, a principle from a martial arts psychology would be best. And that is to be disciplined with your tongue. There is a way to address people by making them feel empowered and respected while getting your point across in a situation like this. You have to make sure that you are using your tongue wisely to avoid escalating the situation any further.

Scenario 3

Someone is doing the pet peeve that you hate. You have asked this person multiple times to stop doing the pet peeve, but they refuse. What should you do to handle this situation?

A. Kindly repeat to them that they are doing what you hate and get them to stop it.
B. Go off and tell them to quit it.
C. Avoid being around them so you do not have to handle it.
D. Practice your stress management skills and kindly tell them that they stop Then, go

about your business whether they stop or not.

Insight: When people trigger your buttons by doing a pet peeve that you hate, it can be tough to hold your tongue or to react favorably. A part of being mentally tough is to stay calm in the middle of being uncomfortable but handle it with grace and resolve so you can get out the situation unharmed according to military psychology. Whatever you do in this situation, you want to make sure that you face the problem head-on and in a respectful way. Ultimately, you will want to weigh your reaction against the whole scheme of things by being self-aware to determine if this is a battle worth picking or not.

Visualizing Day-To-Day Scenarios

Now, it is your turn! In some situations, there is nothing that you can do to prepare yourself for it.

You just have to hope that your mental toughness muscle has been fine-tuned to handle the situation. Some tips to keep in mind when handling situations that you are not prepared:

- Be self-aware. You cannot underestimate the importance of being self-aware in situations. Sometimes, you are so upset with someone else, that you forget to remember, that you are the cause of the problem. If you are self-aware, you are able to quickly understand all the moving parts of a complex situation and be more inclined to make the best decision.

- Do not be a crybaby. Besides the fact that most people do not like a cry-baby, if you only whine about an unfavorable situation when it happens to you, you will be too busy in the pity party that you are not facing the issue. By facing the issue directly and head-on, you have a better chance of getting the results that you want. Even if you do not get the results that you want, by facing the issue head-on, you can address the issue and put your attention to more important things that you are interested in.

- Make sure your expectations are flexible. Sometimes, things do not always happen the way we want to figure out how you can adjust and respond to it in a fast manner, so you can keep going. Remember, just because you have to change your expectations does not mean that you are a failure. It merely means that you are responsive and handle the curveballs that life sends you. And just in case you forgot, being responsive to situations is a sure sign of being mentally tough.

- Transform your negative thoughts. A wise man once said that all good things that happen are not good and all things that happen that are bad are not bad. This means that you need to learn to see the good in negative situations. When you turn back all the layers of a negative situation, what are the positive gems hidden deep down inside?

- Stay calm under pressure. The saying goes that pressure busts pipes or makes diamonds. When you are calm under pressure, you only allow your mind to be mentally clear as possible in order to make the most effective decision possible. Common tips to stay calm under pressure include breathing in and out in stressful situations and counting to ten before you respond to anything.

- Be ethical and courageous. Mentally tough people are courageous. When we think of our most famous leaders, many of them had the mental toughness and were not afraid to take a stand for something they believe in. They were also not afraid to take a stand even when other people were not taking a stand. Oftentimes, the ethical part is overlooked, but mentally tough people know that they can treat others the way they want to be treated and get what they want to accomplish at the same time.

- When you are handling situations, make sure that your reaction aligns with your goals and values. You do not have to do something because you feel pressured. Do not be afraid to say no as it can help you align with your true goals and purpose in life if a decision is not right for you.

- Do not be overwhelmed when you are setting out to become more mentally tough. The best part about any big task is that you can break down tough tasks little bit by little bit. You may not handle one huge thing at one time, but you can handle a huge thing step-by-step or a little bit at a time.

- It is very important to keep in mind your visualization exercises when you are trying to handle scenarios that require you to be mentally tough. If you have something that keeps happening over and over again, meditate and journal about the situation. Then, visualize your reaction to it and the outcome that you want to happen so when the situation happens you are able to handle it well. Remember, to be as detailed as possible with your visualization for the most favorable results.

And, there you have it! These scenarios are giving you the chance to practice your mental toughness muscle and can prepare you for any tough situation that happens in life. We believe in you and we know that you can be mentally tough all the best.

Conclusion

Thank you for making it through to the end of *Mental Toughness!* Let's hope it was informative and able to provide you with all of the tools you need to achieve your goals whatever they may be.

The next step is to prepare yourself for your new path into mental toughness. You now have all the tools that you need to be strong in the mind. Now, maximize them to the best of your ability!

Do you need to create a support system or to reach out to a therapist? Do so! Do you need to buy a journal to start noticing your trends and patterns? Then, do so! Do you need to create your 'why' missions statement? Then, do so! There is no reason for you not to be mentally tough. No more procrastination. Get started as soon as you put this book down!

www.ingramcontent.com/pod-product-compliance
Lightning Source LLC
Chambersburg PA
CBHW071354080526
44587CB00017B/3104